Adelaide Books Children's Literature and Illustration Award

Anthology 2020

Children's Literature and Illustration Award
ANTHOLOGY
2020

Adelaide Books
New York / Lisbon
2021

ANTHOLOGY 2020
By the WINNERS, SHORTLIST WINNER NOMINEES, AND FINALISTS
of the Adelaide Books Children's Literature and Illustration Award Contest

Copyright © by Adelaide Books LLC
Cover image by Elton D'Sousa

Published by Adelaide Books, New York / Lisbon
adelaidebooks.org

Editor: Adelaide Franco Nikolic

For any information, please address Adelaide Books
at info@adelaidebooks.org or write to:
Adelaide Books
244 Fifth Ave. Suite D27
New York, NY, 10001

ISBN: 978-1-955196-13-0

Printed in the United States of America

2nd Annual Contest
ADELAIDE BOOKS
CHILDREN'S LITERATURE
& ILLUSTRATION AWARD
2020

WINNERS

Adelaide Books
Announces the
WINNERS, SHORTLIST WINNER NOMINEES, AND FINALISTS
of the Adelaide Books Children's Literature and Illustration Award,
2nd Annual Contest 2020

BEST CHILDREN'S STORY CATEGORY:

The Winner:

IF I MET THE MOON AT NIGHT by Julie Reed

BEST CHILDREN'S ILLUSTRATION CATEGORY:

The Winner:

Elton D'Sousa

BEST CHILDREN'S STORY CATEGORY

Shortlist Winner Nominees:

A SONG OF STORMS by Lazaro Mariano Perez

BUILDING A BEST FRIEND by Devon Flynn

A NINE-TAILED FOX SISTER by Marianne Song

Finalists:

THE REFRIGERATOR GHOST by Christina Petrides

TUMBLESTEED by Brian Michael Riley

THE MYSTERY BIRD by Andre L. DeCuir

BEST CHILDREN'S ILLUSTRATION CATEGORY

Shortlist Winner Nominees:

Marianne Song

Tammy Bohlens

Joana Marinho

Editor's Note

By Adelaide Franco Nikolic

It was a great satisfaction to organize **The Second Adelaide Books Children's Literature and Illustration Award Competition.**

Considering that 2020 was a challenging year, it was especially rewarding to receive such a big variety of stories and illustrations. Now, more than ever, it is important to bring to light great works that will encourage the smaller ones to develop their love for reading and books.

This anthology gathers what we consider the best submissions. We hope that these illustrations and stories will bring joy to you and your little ones.

Enjoy!

Adelaide

"A children's story that can only be enjoyed by children is not a good children's story in the slightest." —C.S. Lewis

If I Met the Moon at Night

By Julie Reed

If I met the moon at night,
I'd thank her for her pale blue light.
On icy pond set in the snow,
I'd skate for her; she'd smile and glow.

Then I'd ask the twinkling star,
"How do you hang there from afar?
With sticky glue? Or by a string?"
My wish-filled dreams your twinkle brings.

In the forest, calm and dark,
The fireflies will flash and spark.
Like a million lights aglow,
They'll show my path each way I go.

I'll sit with Owl high in the tree,
And hum to him; he'll hoot for me.
And stretch his wings out far and wide,
Then take me on a moonlit ride.

With Toad I'll show how high I hop,
On water's edge, we'll splash and flop.
Then when I tell my favorite joke,
He'll laugh with his big-bellied croak.

On lily pad I'll sit and smile,
As Beaver builds his muddy pile.
He'll work for hours, each stick placed right,
Then SMACK his tail with all his might!

With Fawn through fields I'll run and prance,
We'll make the tall grass sway and dance.
When we reach the hilltop high,
My outstretched arms will hug the sky.

At last with red-haired Fox I walk,
We share kept secrets as we talk.
She tells me all the reasons why
She's charming, crafty, smart, and sly.

And when this evening playtime ends,
I'll wave goodbye to all my friends.
Now off to sleep and dream I might
Of when we'll meet again at night.

I live in Cincinnati, Ohio, with my husband Teague and three children, Mae, Stella, and Mac. When I'm not in my garden, playing music, or taking pictures, I enjoy sharing my imagination and sense of wonder in the stories I write for little listeners. My first picture book, *Stella's Umbrellas* will be published in May 2021 by Adelaide Publishing.

Elton D'Souza is a visual artist from Perth, Australia. He creates illustrations, comics, and 2D animated short films inspired by adventure, fantasy, dragons, and architecture.

LOOKING OUT MY WINDOW by Elton D'Souza

A SONG OF STORMS

By L. M. Perez

There once was a land with a thousand hamlets and in one of the hamlets there were a thousand huts and in one of the huts there lived a boy with no name.

A great misery had befallen the hamlet. The rivulets that ran through it had dried out long ago. There were no fish and no crops, so the people had but scraps to eat. Everyone blamed their misfortune on the boy, for the drought had arrived with his birth. His parents were so ashamed, they didn't give him a name.

The boy had nothing but the clothes on his back and a *shamisen*. "Your grandmother was a *goze,* a traveling musician. She called herself Grasshopper," his father told him once. "That old thing has been to every hamlet in the land and beyond. It has seen the lords and their castles and even lands filled with snow and silver and gold."

The boy, amazed by his grandmother's travels, taught himself how to play the shamisen. He'd go around the hamlet singing happy songs and playing the three-stringed instrument. He dreamed of traveling the land like Grasshopper and making a fortune that would make his parents proud enough to name him, for in the Land of a Thousand Hamlets he who did not have a name was cursed to become an animal.

One day the boy woke up and found gills on his neck. "A fish, I'll turn into a fish," he lamented. He begged his parents to name him but they refused. The boy then decided he'd leave that cursed land like Grasshopper had. He'd play his music for lords and ladies and make a fortune. All his dreams shattered when he found his *shamisen*; its strings had been cut.

"We're sorry, boy. It's just that … we're so very hungry," his parents said.

The boy grabbed his shamisen and ran and ran and ran. He ran until he was surrounded by bamboo. He wandered in the forest until he heard a voice. "Help," it echoed. The boy followed the voice into a pond; he swam deep inside and came out at a grotto.

"Help this one, boy," said a giant koi fish, flailing his tail about. He made the whole grotto tremble. His scales were translucent like water and his whiskers long and shiny like silk threads.

"How did you end up here?" Asked the boy, realizing how hungry he was.

"If the nosey boy must know, this one is a Wind Fish who carries the rain from cloud to cloud," said the pale fish. "This one was bringing rain to this land when he followed the wrong cloud and ended up here. He has become too fat with years of rain. Now he is trapped here."

The boy laughed so hard a tear came out.

"What is funny, hmmm?"

"All these years my people have blamed me for the drought."

"Oh, this one sees it," said the fish, looking at the boy's gills. "The parents didn't give the boy a name out of shame, hmmm?"

The boy nodded bitterly, feeling the gills on his neck.

"Bah, this one will fix it," smiled the Wind Fish, scratching one of his many whiskers with a fin. "All the boy has to do is help this one out of this smelly cave."

The boy agreed. "Though I'm not so sure it's the cave that smells."

They laughed at that.

With much effort, the boy pulled and pushed and rolled the fish into the water. He was too fat to even swim, so the boy had to drag him underwater and pull him out of the pond.

"This one thanks you," said the fish. "Now he will help." He then pulled three of his whiskers and gave them to the boy.

The boy strung his shamisen with the whiskers and began to play one of his songs.

"This one likes you and he likes this song. From now on he will bring the rain whenever you play it. This one must go now." The fish began to float ever so slightly. "Oh, he almost forgot to tell you a secret."

"What?"

The fish whispered the boy's True Name before flying away.

"Keep your True Name safe, boy," he said as he disappeared among the clouds.

The boy waved the fish goodbye. "I have a name," he said with glee. He whispered his True Name to the wind, stopping his transformation into a fish. His gills remained, alas. He walked back to the hamlet and gathered everyone by the dried rivulets. He sang his song, picking at the strings happily. At first, some laughed, some jeered, and some left, but then thunder boomed. A raindrop walked on the boy's shoulder, slid down his shamisen, and crashed into the dry dirt that was once a rivulet. The crowd fell silent. A raindrop followed, then another and another until the hamlet was drenched. The boy didn't stop playing his song until the rivulets flowed once more. Lightning danced madly across the sky and for a brief moment, he thought he heard the thunder gods beating their drums in celebration.

The hamlet grew prosperous thanks to the boy. Everyone apologized for how awful they'd been to him. His parents even offered to name him.

"Thank you," the boy said, bowing to them. "But I must refuse."

The next morning the boy left the hamlet with nothing but the clothes on his back, his shamisen, and his True Name. He called himself Windfish during his travels, for no one should ever know another's True Name.

Without the boy's song, the hamlet fell back into ruin.

L. M. Perez

Lázaro Mariano Pérez was born and raised in Cuba. He moved to the U.S in 2008 and slowly fell in love with writing and telling stories. His Afro-Cuban heritage is a constant influence in his storytelling.

"A nine-tailed fox sister" by Marianne Song

"River in the sunset" by Marianne Song

"Fox in front of the tomb" by Marianne Song

"A straw-house" by Marianne Song

Marianne Song is an essayist who strives to reproduce the feelings and memories with poetic images through English instead of her mother tongue, Korean, to convey her raw emotions as honestly as possible, otherwise might be fabricated by self-consciousness. The way she explores her experiences and memories to correlate with social issues corroborates her viewpoint that arts can be far away from reality. Her education in Switzerland and China expanded her capacity of cultural tolerance arising from different ethnicities. A variety of people she met, talked to, and shared her feelings within two countries gives her artistic inspiration for creative writing and painting.

Based on own memories, she enjoys reinterpreting photos and pictures from newspapers, magazines, and books and express her true emotions. Her writing and paintings are bordered with the nostalgia of her search for the innocence and purity of childhood. The colors are an essential part of the process to fill the inner emptiness arising from the unbridgeable chasm between my desire and reality.

Currently, she is working as a writer and English instructor in Jeju Island, Korea, with an unwavering belief that someday her angst and hardships could be transformed into artistic treasure in the same way the natural wonders of Jeju were made from a volcanic eruption. Whenever facing a big challenge, she quietly whispers to herself 'Don't be afraid, follow your heart.'

BUILDING A BEST FRIEND

by Devon Flynn

Tommy was feeling sad and lonely one day.

"What's wrong?" asked his neighbor Susie, hoping to cheer him up.

"I don't have anyone to do anything with. I don't like being alone," he told her.

"Why don't we build you a best friend?" she suggested.

Tommy's eyes lit up with excitement.

"That's a great idea! Then we can play hide and seek, make forts in the backyard, and do other fun things!"

So off the two went to build Tommy a new best friend.

First they went to the recycling depot.

"If we're going to build a best friend, we're going to need parts!" declared Tommy.

They asked Mr. Jenkins who worked at the recycling depot for advice. He suggested they use cardboard.

"It's light and stackable," he told them. "And it comes in all shapes and sizes too!"

Mr. Jenkins' son, Ben, asked what Tommy and Susie were doing as they searched through a large pile of cardboard.

"We're building Tommy a best friend," replied Susie excitedly.

"Would you like to help?" asked Tommy.

But Ben declined.

"I'd rather ride my bike," he replied and rode away on his shiny red bike.

After searching through almost all the cardboard, Tommy and Susie finally found the perfect parts.

"Now we just need to put him together," said Tommy.

They quickly returned to Tommy's house.

Along the way, they ran into Jacob.

"What are all those boxes and tubes for?" he asked Tommy and Susie.

"We're building Tommy a best friend," said Susie.

"Did you want to help put him together?" asked Tommy.

"Sure," replied Jacob, "I love building things."

There were lots of boxes to choose from and many different ways to assemble a best friend.

"We should start with his legs and then build up," said Susie. "What do you think Jacob?"

But Jacob was preoccupied. Tommy, however, agreed.

"You're right. We can use the long boxes for his legs. Jacob, can you pass me that box?" asked Tommy.

But Jacob wasn't listening. He was busy smashing a tall stack of boxes.

"Should we use cardboard boxes or tubes for his arms?" asked Susie.

But Jacob was no longer interested in helping Tommy build a best friend.

"I'm bored. I'm going home to play video games. Bye!" he said, leaving.

But Tommy and Susie continued working on Tommy's new best friend.

"He just needs to be decorated now," said Tommy excitedly.

"Ooh! I have art supplies at my house. Let's go!"

And off they went next door.

As they returned to Tommy's house with their arms full of glue, glitter, crayons, and stickers, Tommy and Susie met Zachary.

"We're decorating my new best friend," said Tommy.

"Would you like to join us?" asked Susie.

"Sure," said Zachary. "I'm really good at decorating!"

The three went upstairs to Tommy's room and began to decorate his new best friend.

Susie glued glitter, Tommy stuck stickers and Zachary colored with crayons.

"His eyes should be blue, not green," Zachary told Tommy. But blue was Tommy's favorite color.

"His buttons should be smaller," Zachary told Susie. Tommy liked big buttons.

"And he should have lasers!" exclaimed Zachary.

Tommy protested, "But I don't want him to have lasers. I don't want him to have small buttons. And I like blue!"

Zachary wasn't being very helpful.

"Maybe you just don't know robots like I do," he said.

Susie politely suggested Zachary make his own best friend.

"This way, everyone's happy!" she said.

Zachary liked this idea and ran back home to start designing his own best friend.

Tommy and Susie were soon done. Tommy's new best friend looked amazing! He had blue eyes, big buttons, and no lasers. On his front was a large switch that said, "On/Off."

"All you need to do is switch him on," said Susie. "And then you'll have a new best friend!"

Tommy was very excited. He and his best friend would play hide and seek! Make forts! And do other fun things! He was about to hit the switch to turn on his best friend, but he stopped. He thought about everything that happened earlier that day:

Susie had been there to cheer him up…

Susie had suggested building a best friend…

Susie had helped search for parts…

Susie had helped put the best friend together…

Tommy didn't have to build a best friend. He had one all along.

Devon Flynn

I'm a writer of all kinds, living in a small town in northern British Columbia. I'm just hoping my words can find meaning in the right person who reads them.

"Meadow of Melancholia" by Tammy Bohlens

"Midnight Hike" by Tammy Bohlens

"Vampire Bat" by Tammy Bohlens

Tammy Bohlens is an illustrator and storyteller from Hamburg, Germany, where she currently studies and specializes in book illustration. She uses fine ink lines and washes of watercolor to create wondrous worlds that house secrets, adventures, and strange beings from another realm.

A NINE-TAILED FOX SISTER

by Marianne Song

At sunset, the glistening and rolling waves slowly eat the falling sun. When the massive weight of the sun splashes into the water, its golden hues powder the rippling surface of the river where fluffy light -brown reeds grow in abundance. When the sky breathes out slowly, the tall grass reeds bend down just above the water, as if embracing their reflections. It seems like all of nature starts to breathe in and out after that.

A boy with a wide-brimmed hat drags up a net half-filled with rocks with all his might. The shape of his body, which is less than five feet tall, seems to be melting in the sunset. After a long struggle with the heavy net, it thumps down with a splash. Soon it pools around the boat. The loosened net is covered in seaweed and sand. The boy's fingers are busy searching for fish among the seaweed. Sometimes the jagged rocks make scratches on his small hands. "He is still coughing and waiting for my arrival with money," mutters the fisherboy, Dongsoo. Unfortunately, he has to return home empty-handed. He is sad thinking about how he can't sell fish today. Nothing can be earned for today. The shimmering light is dimming more and more.

Dong-soo helplessly rows the boat across the silver waves under the moon. The oars make a squeaking sound as the boat moves toward land. Out of the boat, he trails into the forest. Lined with heavy elm trees whose branches seem to be growing longer and longer to catch him, the path seems to move with the shadows of the trees. The full moon is hanging over the trees, then follows his footsteps. He feels like he's being chased by a gust of wind. The tree spirits seem to be devouring his shadow. Drops of sweat run down his back. It is a chilling moment.

Suddenly, the full moon shines on a little fox scratching at the ground hardening the mound with her claws. The sound of her weeping is drowned out by a swarm of crows screaming loudly. Their noise fills the sky and echoes off trees and rocks. When the little fox notices Dong-soo, it suddenly morphs into a five-year-old girl. Her plaited hair has come loose. "Please help me. I am orphaned. My mom was shot to death by a hunter," cries the little girl. It takes a few minutes for Dong-soo to pull himself together. His trembling voice comes out. "Who are you?" Hesitantly, she casts her eyes upon the moon, then upon Dong-soo, and back again. "My mom is a nine-tailed fox," she says when she opens her mouth, "and I am her baby fox."

Dong-soo remembers what his father told him. Legend has it that a nine-tailed fox can become human if she eats a human's liver. He starts to run off, but she follows him desperately. She pleads through her tears. "I am homeless. I want to be loved like humans. My mom is already dead. I have no one to love and to be loved by. That is nothing more than death." Her bare feet are bleeding, sticky with wet soil. Soon after, she falls over the jagged roots of a tree that have grown upward like a witch's long nail.

A surge of compassion pushes Dong-soo's fear of the nine-tailed fox away and interlocks with his memories of his little sister, who had gone to Heaven already. Momentarily, he imagines his dead sister being reincarnated into this fox girl. "My house has a straw roof that is almost collapsing. I live with my dying father. He coughs day and night. Are you okay with living in such a poor and shabby house with my family?" the boy asks, raising her up. Relief floods her face, her lips lifting toward her eyes. "Is the human bond of family love almost the same as ours? It must be beautiful, warm, and cozy, like the feeling of spring melting away the coldness," the little girl says. Then she transforms into a fox with nine silver-gray tails. "I can no longer follow you in a human body. It's better to be a fox for the time being," she continues. They leave behind the footsteps of a human and a fox, and falling leaves quickly hide their traces.

Down the slopes of mountains on their journey home, there is a pond where the willow branches hang low, like a couple that's going to embrace each other. The long arms of the willows seem to reach for the ripples in the pool. The trees and water are breathing in and out together. Once Dong-soo's sister liked to hold the trunks of the willows in her arms tightly to call the tree spirits. The wind shakes the leaves slowly. She seems to be turning green. "Now she's not here anymore." Dong-soo is sharing his childhood memories with the baby fox, his new sister. "I had to be a grown-up quickly to sustain a life, which was a burden to me." The baby fox looks at him for a moment, and gradually, she feels connected to his loneliness. A bubble of compassion rises in her heart, as she knows what death means. Dong-soo asks, "Will you live as my younger sister together with me even though my house is so old and small? I will protect you as your elder brother." Being together is what she wants to hear now that she is orphaned. She used to share every hour of every day and night with her mother. 'No matter how poverty-stricken the house looks, to the extent that it could be under piles of snow or it could be flooded by heavy rain, it's okay as long as he cares for me and I care for him.' She follows him with her nine tails wagging.

Upon arriving home with the little girl, before entering the room, Dong-soo cautions her, "Do not come into the room until I call you in." She blinks in an attempt to say yes. He slides the lattice door open to check if his father is asleep. His blank eyes, sunken above high cheekbones, are looking at the ceiling. The moldy corner of his smelly room seems to be coming down toward his face. It is almost as if he is waiting for death as a savior to end his dreary life. An air of dread hangs around him like a web.

Staring down at his shrunken body, which looks like a dried fish, Dong-soo wants to have the old days back, when he was surrounded by his mom and sister. 'Is it possible for a nine-tailed fox sister to bring happiness back to me?' He sighs again hopelessly. 'No one, not even a blind man, wants to live here.' He props his feeble father up against the wall to feed him a bowl of rice porridge. Although he doesn't think his dad can hear him, he shares with him what he went through in the evening after gathering mussels. The moment Dong-soo mentions the nine-tailed fox, his father's blind eyes widen. Abruptly, he blurts out, "If I drink its blood and chew its liver, I will recover from this severe pneumonia. Please get it for me!" He pleads over and over. His body language screams how desperate he is. Dong-soo loves his dad too. His heart is pounding loudly. He doesn't know what to do.

In the meantime, Mi-hua, the baby fox, is curiously looking at the silhouettes reflected on the papered sliding door. She wonders how it is to live with human beings. Suddenly, the spirit of her mother appears in the night fog. The mouth of the white fox with nine tails opens slowly. "Never believe humans. Their minds change like day and night. They will surely harm you. Their promise of protection is easily broken. I asked a mole couple to dig a hole under the fireplace for you. When the humans lock you in the kitchen, use the hole to escape them." When Dong-soo opens the door to call Mi-hua, the ghost fox slowly vanishes into the darkness.

The nine-tailed baby fox, Mi-hua, wants to believe Dong-soo is her human brother. His eyes and voice have a warmth like her mother's. She shakes her head, unbelieving. 'Dong-soo will protect me, as promised. He is different from other humans.'

Dong-soo comes up to her to introduce her to his father. She transforms into a little girl and dresses herself with a long skirt to hide her nine tails. In the eyes of Dong-soo, she looks lovely, just like his sister. However, nothing is more urgent than saving his father, because he is a good son. Besides, she is not human; she is just an animal. He tries to force a smile, in the guise of kindness. "Mi-hua, could you get my father a bowl of water, please? He is coughing so hard. There is a kitchen next to the gate." He plans to lock her inside and then make smoke to suffocate her. He wants to believe that his betrayal of his nine-tailed fox sister can be justified by saving his father. The spirit of his eyes begins to dim. He imagines the ferryman of death coming closer to take him to the underworld. Mi-hua's genial eyes meet his without any doubt before she goes to get a bowl of water. Dong-soo knows that animals never play a double game when they trust humans. The selfishness of humans can lock their conscience away and then turn them into monsters.

Mi-hua takes a deep bow before his father and leans him against the wall to serve him water. Then she rubs his face carefully with a soaked towel. Her sincere attempt to be human moves Dong-soo's heart. What he fears most is the thought of killing the beautiful and pure Mi-hua, even though she is a nine-tailed fox. He suddenly goes out to calm himself down. The yarns of compassion and pity toward the orphaned Mi-hua are woven into his heart, and they tighten around it. He feels the wooden strength of the forest, the stillness of the sky, and the darkness of the soil start to encircle him. To his eyes, the crescent moon has transformed into a narrow eye looking down at him. All of nature's wonder is watching him quietly. He decides to give Mi-hua beautiful memories, if possible, before sending her back to where she came from—that is, nature.

The next day, he presents a rainbow-striped jacket and a red skirt to her. "Mi-hua, these clothes are for tomorrow's moon festival. Our neighbors will go up to the hill hemmed in by valleys and craggy mountains to pray for happiness under the moonlight. We will form a circle by holding hands, and we will whirl. We will become a large spinning wheel. We will sing a song of Ganggangsullae (circling wheel). I guess you have never tried it before. I will wash your clothes and comb your hair into a long braid. You will surely be an amazing girl." Dong-soo smiles at her, wishing to leave a beautiful memory as a farewell present to Mi-hua. This will act as a bridge between him and her no matter how far and how long they will be separated. While their eyes are locked, he slowly confesses. "My beloved sister, Mi-hua, you have to leave here after the festival, then go deep into the forest where you used to live. Otherwise, my ailing dad will kill you to save his life." He starts to weep over the farewell with Mi-hua. She nods. "I overheard what your father told you. I am so pleased that you didn't betray me."

When the full moon has risen above the valleys and mountains to listen to the neighbors' wishes, Mi-hua, the nine-tailed baby fox, joins the dancing wheel of girls, who hold her hands tightly as a welcoming gesture. Mi-hua's red silk skirt flutters in the autumn wind. The air is crisp and chilling to their cheeks, turning them a pinkish hue. In the middle of the circle, hands interlocked with each other, the flames are also dancing under the moon. There are millions of fireflies all around them, blinking at different rates. This is more than a starry night in the eyes of this baby fox, who used to howl at the moon with her mom.

The moon festival culminates in the procession of baskets of autumn fruits, pigs smoked over a fire, and dried fish, which break the dancing wheel, one after another. They were being carried by men. While Dong-soo and Mi-hua enjoy one bite after another, sharing these moments, he wishes that these memories will be frozen between the past and present for Mi-hua. Then he gives her the signal to leave. She disappears into the darkness. After a while, a howling sound echoes from far away. It must be Mi-hua, his nine-tailed fox sister.

A few days later, Dong-soo notices wild ginseng lying in front of the entrance to his house. It is considered an elixir plant, and it will surely heal his father. He knows Mi-hua left it in return for him saving her life. He believes the memories with Mi-hua will unite them forever.

"Kiki" by Joana Cristina Nascimento Marinho

"Kiki" by Joana Cristina Nascimento Marinho
(a draft)

Joana Cristina Nascimento Marinho was born on 11th July 1999, in Porto, the northern Portuguese city where she grew up and currently lives. Ever since she was a little girl she has always loved the characters in the books that surrounded her, having as favourite literary genres the Portuguese and Anglo-Saxon classics and graphic novels. A lover of other arts, she also dedicates herself, in her spare time, to painting, an art in which she already has two masterpieces. Currently, preserving her inclination in literature, and aiming to professionally teach the two languages she most dominates – Portuguese and English –, she is completing her degree in Languages, Literatures and Cultures at the Faculty of Arts of the University of Porto, where she will continue her studies for two more years. In the meantime, she writes mysterious short stories that take her most intriguing and mesmerizing dreams as their starting point.

THE REFRIGERATOR GHOST

by Christina Petrides

"I could have sworn there was another piece of chicken!" Mom said, opening the refrigerator. "But there's no chicken here. We must have a ghost!"

"Sweetie, where's the mustard?" asked Dad, looking into the refrigerator.

"It's right in front of you," Mom answered. "On the second shelf."

"I don't see it," Dad said. He closed the door.

Mom opened the refrigerator door again. "It's right there, where I said it was!"

"It wasn't there a second ago," Dad said. "We must have a ghost."

"Sam, did you eat that pie I made for the class party?" shouted Jessica.

"No, sis," he said.

"Well, I know Dad and Mom didn't eat it. And it's gone now," Jessica yelled. "You must've eaten it!"

"I didn't!" Sam said. "It must've been a ghost."

Jessica didn't believe him. And she was right. Sam had eaten the pie.

But Sam and Dad and Mom were also right, although they didn't know it. The Tomason family had a ghost. A refrigerator ghost.

Now, ghosts don't live in every refrigerator. Some people have clean refrigerators. But when lots of food gets lost and or spilled on the shelves, a refrigerator ghost will sometimes appear.

The Tomason's refrigerator was a mess.

The Tomason's ghost didn't like living in their refrigerator. The shelves were crowded and the smell was terrible. But a refrigerator ghost can't disappear until old food does. And the more rotten, stinky stuff sits on the shelves, the bigger the ghost gets.

Many people think ghosts are scary, but the Tomason's refrigerator ghost was not scary. In fact, it was afraid of people. So, it hid behind milk cartons and fruit and leftovers.

The ghost was always cold and tired, too. It couldn't even sleep at night, because Sam and Jessica liked to have midnight snacks and Mom and Dad got up early to eat breakfast and go to work. It woke up whenever the refrigerator door was opened and the light turned on. So, the poor ghost shivered and yawned and sniffled and sneezed all the time.

The ghost dreamed of being free, and of sunshine and fresh air. But the Tomason's refrigerator got more and more full of forgotten food. The refrigerator ghost was trapped.

"We ought to clean out the fridge," Dad said. But he was too busy.

"We've got to clean out the fridge," said Mom. But she was too busy.

Finally, one Friday night, Sam and Jessica both came looking for a midnight snack at the same time. They opened the refrigerator. They both screamed.

Mom and Dad came running out of their room. "What? What happened?" they asked. "Did you see a ghost?"

No. They didn't. They all saw and smelled the refrigerator.

"It's just nasty!" Jessica gasped.

"It smells like something died in there," Sam gagged.

The ghost was insulted. It hadn't made the refrigerator dirty. That was the Tomason's fault!

"Enough is enough," Mom and Dad agreed. "We're going to clean out the refrigerator first thing in the morning."

So, on Saturday, the Tomasons took everything out of the refrigerator. They washed the shelves, and put the good food back inside, along with a packet of baking soda to get rid of lingering smells. They carried all the expired food out to their new compost bin in the back yard.

Soon, the refrigerator ghost wasn't a refrigerator ghost any longer. It was a compost bin ghost. The compost bin was big and warm. And because there wasn't an electric light in the bin, the ghost quickly fell asleep. When the Tomason's added more food scraps after dinner every night, this didn't wake him up.

And slowly, all that nasty old food turned into fertilizer, which didn't really stink. It smelled like earth.

In the spring, the Tomasons planted a garden. They put their compost fertilizer in the garden to help the plants grow.

And each day, a really happy breeze wandered through the new flowers and vegetables, breathing fresh air and soaking up the sunshine. It hoped it would never become a refrigerator ghost again!

Born in Texas and raised in the Central Savannah River Area (CSRA) of Georgia, United States, **Christina E. Petrides** has lived and worked on Jeju Island, Republic of Korea, since 2017. Her first children's book, *Blueberry Man*, was published by Tchaikovsky Family Books in May 2020. Her poetry has been published in more than a score of periodicals. She co-translated Maria Shelyakhovskaya's *Utverzhdenie v liubvi. Istoria odnoi russkoi sem'i: 1872-1981 (Being Grounded in Love: A History of One Russian Family, 1872-1981)*, the English version of which remains in manuscript.

TUMBLESTEED

by Brian Michael Riley

Cross them plains so gold 'n great, back in the days of old and late,
A little tumbleweed went tumblin' for tumblin' seemed this weed's fate.

No moss its branches gathered as criss-crossed such ranches scattered
Went this tumblin' weed or stumblin' or just fumblin' if it rathered.

But then came that confoundin' day when the houndin' wind insisted
Our weed swish this way and twist and sway 'til of a mystery it consisted.

Cuz nestled nice and tight inside that nest of bristly thistles
Was a homely dome of ghostly bone and wide, white smile of whistles.

Thus hindered by this inner burden our bramble went hobblin'
'Til coughing up that noggin to the crust where it came bobbin'.

And then from someplace deep inside that craggy, jagged grin
A silly, shrilly, chilling voice implored this whinnied din:

"Oh woe the end is neigh, I bray, here walloped with such luck,
"As long gone are my ways of play while galloping amok!

"For my here my head hangs dangled on this tangled, mangled hide,
"And with this thorny mane I mourn how now I cannot ride!"

To all this grumbling our just tumbling friend shook an amends
And whisked them quick and nifty to *Biff's Thrifty Odds 'n Ends*.

As there was stocked a rocking horse they knocked clear off its crooks
Then hopped atop to bop and rock but of its knack they never took.

"Ack!" the head hacked to the back, complaining of that rack,
"I'm a horse not born for boards adorned with wood stain and shellac!"

So off they went on rollin' to the seasonal state fair
Patrollin' within reason for what stake they might claim there.

And that was where they heard a tinny, jingling type of sound
With a pristine ring of pole-pierced ponies prancing round and round.

While parked and harking right beside this was a barking man
Who drew two tickets from our twosome into his tin can.

So that up one shiny post could bound the skull and windy host
But for this scary, barely merry going around there rose no boast.

Rather, "Whoah," the skull bemoaned of their new madcap mobile home,
"I've nil the will for such frills and thrills when once chromosomes to roam!"

So our musty, dusty, gusted cluster mustered up the mettle
To mine a find defined as fine by that mind atop its nettles.

Thus rebounding out the roundabout 'til sounder ground was found
Complete with clean neat streets and pleated greens and tweeting trees abound.

And oh how quaint and saintly was the scene 'til meanly tainted
By a queer offense beside a picket fence to which our heroes nearly fainted.

For there were vendor-rented party tents and vats of bright cuisine
Filled with the snaps of caps and pointed hats on screaming tykes and tweens.

While mixed within these kids with sticks - with which they'd turned quite savage -
Was a divine equine fixed up with twine being whipped and churned 'til ravaged.

Then with horror came aborted from the Trojan's torn midsection
An assortment of confections pouring forth in all directions.

"Oh what carnage!" gasped the quaking cap on its shrub of shivers,
"Upon this plot we cannot trot if onslaught it delivers!"

And to this hoot, which drew those brutes toward gruesome new abuse,
Was a racing chase out the gates of our disgraced face and roots caboose!

'Til tossed across plains gold and great back near where we began
Our little tumbleweed with a steed in its pedigree bumbled back again.

And as our frazzled, raveled travelers bounded through those parts
An astounding pounding sounded out 'cross the ground into their hearts.

"Hi ho!" bellowed our lonesome bone upon its roaming coach,
"Such thunderous tones this soul beholds as a brothers' toes approach!"

As coursing down the concourse came a raging horse cascade
Which stormed upon our decayed suede and aid 'til torn and frayed.

For smacked and cracked that bush was whacked by all the hoof to-do
'Til doubly crumbled was our duo and left split in two.

But as the tempest pressed on westward in its rusty gusts
From the battalion soared a stallion with a stardust thrust.

And though torn asunder our born tumbler dared it was in bloom
For what a blast at last to grasp its pal that passed go zoom!

Brian Michael Riley is a writer, illustrator and multimedia artist living in California's Bay Area with his girlfriend and many, many pets.

THE MYSTERY BIRD
A Tale of the Ivory-Billed Woodpecker
by Andre L. DeCuir

Around Great-Grandma and Great-Grandpa's bayou home, there is much to see. There could be a possum under the azalea bushcs. There could be a frog on the back porch. Of course, there are plenty of birds . . . except one. Maybe.

Every morning, Great-Grandpa heads to the bayou, even before the coffee is made. He's always back just as Great-Grandma is serving up the *beignets* for breakfast.

"Paw-Paw," where do you go every morning?" I ask.

Great-Grandma looks at Great-Grandpa and says, "Tell your story, Paw-Paw."

Great-Grandpa sits at the table, smiles, and takes a small piece of paper out of his pocket. It looks old, ragged around the edges, and full of creases. There is a sketch of a bird on it with a thick beak and a large, round eye. The red color on the top of the head is faded but still noticeable. Only the tops of the white, outstretched wings are shaded black.

"I go out to look for birds like this fellow—the ivory-billed woodpecker."

"That should be easy. There are a lot of birds around here."

"Not this one. It's believed to be extinct. Do you know what that means?"

"It's not around anymore?"

Great-Grandpa nods.

"A long time ago, these old swamps around here used to be full of them, but because of the cutting down of trees, the bird has become extinct—or almost extinct. There have been reports of some sightings now and then, in different places, but no one is sure if this particular woodpecker was actually seen."

"Tell about that drawing, Paw-Paw," urges Great-Grandma as she pours glasses of milk.

"I saw the ivory-billed woodpecker back in 1944 when I was little like you are now, and I made that drawing. Now, I keep going out every morning, hoping to catch a glimpse of one."

"Can I go with you tomorrow?"

"Paw-Paw goes out really early, *Cher*," says Great-Grandma.

"I can be ready!"

"*Bien!* Tomorrow morning then, we'll go out looking for the ivory-billed woodpecker," says Great-Grandpa. "Maybe you'll be my good luck charm!"

Early the next morning, we walk through the fog along the bayou until we come to an old wooden chair set under some cottonwoods. Great-Grandpa wipes it off with his sleeve.

"Is this where you watch for the ivory-billed woodpecker, Paw-Paw?"

"Yes it is, but you can get up in the chair if you want."

"Where do we look?"

"Well, the best thing to do is to listen first. The ivory-billed woodpecker makes a loud, quick, double knocking sound when it pecks at a tree. Like this."

"Bap-bap" is the sound Pop-Pop makes with his knuckles against the wooden chair. "It also makes a high-pitched call that sounds something like a toy horn you might toot at a birthday party."

I curl up in the chair and fall asleep.

The ivory-billed woodpecker then flies from the crumpled drawing and into dreams, answering the question "Where are you?" in funny, silly ways.

Maybe it is hiding in Great-Grandma's old crawfish pot, where she makes many a tasty *etoufee.*

Maybe it is hiding in Mr. Degroux's *magasin* where he sells the best ice cream, perfect on a hot, summer day.

Maybe it is hiding in Mrs. Fournier's roses, all red, yellow, and white.

Maybe it is hiding in the old plantation house, peeking through dark windows, like ghosts do at night.

"BAP-bap!"

"Listen! Listen!" says Great-Grandpa.

"BAP-bap!" comes the sound again, a fast double knock.

"I thought you were dozing off on me," says Great-Grandpa with a smile.

"Sorry, Paw-Paw. Is that the woodpecker?"

"It sure sounds like it. Now we look around for it."

From somewhere comes a sound that doesn't seem made by anything real.

Kinnnnt, kinnnt!

Then it happens.

"Paw-Paw! Look!"

A large bird flies just under the trees along the bayou and then swoops up into the cypresses, finally disappearing into the green leaves and moss. It looks like the bird in the little drawing, black, with white along the bottom edges of the wings, and the crest, a splash of red.

"Was that it? Was that it?"

"I believe it was," says Great-Grandpa. "I knew you would be my good luck charm!"

We walk back to the house, and Great-Grandpa asks, "You know that little drawing I gave you?"

"Uh-huh."

"Well, it's yours now. You saw the ivory-billed woodpecker, and now the drawing is yours to keep."

The drawing is always with me when I visit Great-Grandpa and Great -Grandma. We go out to that old wooden chair along the bayou, we listen, and we look into the tall cypress trees, hoping to get another glimpse of the mystery bird, the ivory-billed woodpecker.

Andre DeCuir teaches at Muskingum University in New Concord, Ohio. His work has appeared in publications such as *Adelaide Literary Magazine, Blink-Ink, Heron Tree, Mystery Tribune,* and *Shotgun Honey.*

Lightning Source UK Ltd.
Milton Keynes UK
UKHW051900120421
381859UK00002B/201